First World War
and Army of Occupation
War Diary
France, Belgium and Germany

59 DIVISION
Divisional Troops
467 Field Company Royal Engineers
1 November 1915 - 27 February 1916

WO95/3017/1

The Naval & Military Press Ltd
www.nmarchive.com
Published in association with The National Archives

Published by

The Naval & Military Press Ltd

Unit 10 Ridgewood Industrial Park,

Uckfield, East Sussex,

TN22 5QE England

Tel: +44 (0) 1825 749494

www.naval-military-press.com

www.nmarchive.com

This diary has been reprinted in facsimile from the original. Any imperfections are inevitably reproduced and the quality may fall short of modern type and cartographic standards.

© **Crown Copyright**
Images reproduced by permission of The National Archives, London, England, 2015.

Contents

Document type	Place/Title	Date From	Date To
Heading	WO95/3017/1		
Heading	War Diary Of 59 Division 467 Coy Regt Formerly 1/3 N Mid Fld Coy RE 1915 Nov-1916 Feb		
Heading	War Diary Of 1/3rd North Midland Field Co. R.E. From 1st November, 1915. To 23 January, 1916.		
War Diary	Radlett	01/11/1915	20/11/1915
War Diary	Shenley	29/11/1915	23/01/1916
Heading	War Diary Of 1/3rd N.M. Field Coy RE. From February 1st 1916 To February 29th 1916. (Volume 1)		
War Diary	Park Street	02/02/1916	02/02/1916
War Diary	Shenley	10/02/1916	23/02/1916
War Diary	Brightlingsea	27/02/1916	27/02/1916

WO95/3017/-

59 DIVISION

467 COY RES

formerly
1/3 N MID FLD COY RE

1915 NOV — 1916 FEB

CONFIDENTIAL.

WAR DIARY

of

1/3RD NORTH MIDLAND FIELD CO. R.E.

From 1st November, 1915.   To 23rd January, 1916.

Army Form C. 2118.

WAR DIARY
or
INTELLIGENCE SUMMARY.
(Erase heading not required.)

Instructions regarding War Diaries and Intelligence Summaries are contained in F.S. Regs., Part II. and the Staff Manual respectively. Title pages will be prepared in manuscript.

Hour, Date, Place	Summary of Events and Information	Remarks and references to Appendices
Received.		
1st November 1915. RADLETT.	Authority for moving 1/3 North Midland Field Co from a' company a' Northern command from YORK.	P.B.7
6th November 1915	County Associations of DERBYSHIRE, NOTTINGHAMSHIRE and LEICESTERSHIRE informed by C.R.E. and O.C. 1/3 field Co. during month-end.	P.B.7
20th November 1915	Company 136 strong now attached owing to reservists & time's air SHENLEY to RADLETT.	P.B.7
29th November 1915. SHENLEY	An advance party attached to 2/2 and 3/1 field Co. at RADLETT for instruction in noting and training in mounted duties as 1/3 field Co. had no horses.	P.B.7

(9 29 6) W 3332—1107 100,000 10/13 H W V Forms/C. 2118/10.

Army Form C. 2118.

WAR DIARY
or
INTELLIGENCE SUMMARY.
(Erase heading not required.)

Instructions regarding War Diaries and Intelligence Summaries are contained in F. S. Regs., Part II. and the Staff Manual respectively. Title pages will be prepared in manuscript.

Hour, Date, Place	Summary of Events and Information	Remarks and references to Appendices
6th December 1915. SHENLEY	Company arms received strength 4 & 213.	D.B.9.
20th December 1915. SHENLEY.	Inspection of R.E. huts at RADLETT by Brig. Gen. ROPER. The mens & the 1/3 Field Co. were inspected in their huts. RADLETT camp now being taken over by 2/3 and 3/1 Co. The wagons of 1/3 Co. were inspected at SHENLEY.	D.B.9.

Army Form C. 2118.

WAR DIARY
or
INTELLIGENCE SUMMARY.
(Erase heading not required.)

Instructions regarding War Diaries and Intelligence Summaries are contained in F. S. Regs., Part II. and the Staff Manual respectively. Title pages will be prepared in manuscript.

Hour, Date, Place	Summary of Events and Information	Remarks and references to Appendices
18th January 1916. SHENLEY.	2nd war. war to G.O.C. 59th Bris. who came & chatty and saw men at work.	P.B.7
23rd January 1916 SHENLEY.	Hman recd of Strength of 59 and an draw in recruits from RADLETT to do duty with this Co.	P.B.9.

Confidential

War Diary

of

1/3rd N.M. FIELD COY R.E.

From February 1st 1916 to February 29th 1916.

(Volume 1)

Instructions regarding War Diaries and Intelligence Summaries are contained in F. S. Regs., Part II. and the Staff Manual respectively. Title pages will be prepared in manuscript.

WAR DIARY 1/3 North Mid. Field Co. R.E. Army Form C. 2118.
or
INTELLIGENCE SUMMARY.
(Erase heading not required.)

1/3 North Mid. Field Co. R.E.

Hour, Date, Place	Summary of Events and Information	Remarks and references to Appendices
2nd January 1916 PARK STREET	Lieut. Gen. Sir A.E. CODRINGTON witnessed pon. Route March near Park Street.	P.B.9.
10th January 1916 SHENLEY	Col. GRANT C.E. 3rd Army saw men at work at SHENLEY.	P.B.9.
18th January 1916 SHENLEY	Maj. Gen. A.E. SANDBACH visited to inspect men at work.	P.B.9.
23rd January 1916 SHENLEY	W.E. Parr VIII now appears to run down. See D.O. 339.	P.B.9.
27th January 1916 BRIGHTLINGSEA	Proceeded with Co. under orders to BRIGHTLINGSEA for a month course of Pontooning and Heavy Bridging.	P.B.9.

D.B. Grew O.C.
Major (per return)